# letters i'll never send

arlyne soto

# dedication

to anyone still working
through their trauma.
I see you.
you are not alone.

## disclaimer


The poems in this book cover some details
of my traumatic experience in an abusive relationship,
these include topics such as self-harm and physical/
sexual assault.


Please take moments for self-care
as needed while you read these poems.

# TABLE OF CONTENTS

**I'm scared.**

I'm scared about the future,
my mental health,
the end result of my current relationship.
I know you told me and said some hurtful things.
That's not okay.
And you know that.
I believe so.
The first time it happened I was hoping was the last.
But, it wasn't.
Less than a month later,
we were back at it again.
But, I don't want that to happen anymore,
I didn't want there to be a first time or a second time
or a last time.
I didn't want it to happen ever.
And well it did.
And here we are.
And here I am scared that nothing will change.
Things will always be this way.
Things are good now, but what about later?
What if you or I or we get so angry
and worked up that everything just collapses?

Then do we say our goodbyes?
I don't think I would be able to continue anymore.
If the hurtful behavior continues.
It's like every small argument we get into
makes me think it's going to happen all over again.
I know you're trying but please change for you.
Not for me.
I change to make myself better and happier.
I want you to do the same for yourself.
And I think you are.
I know I need to make changes.
I had let sides of me show that I never thought
would be shown.
And that actually makes me a little sad,
makes me a little worried.
But, it also means that I am not perfect either.
That I have my limits.
That I don't want to be held down.
I don't want to be disrespected.
And now you know that if anything
like that happens again,
you will lose me.

I am not going to try again.
Twice is already one too many.
I don't want this to be over.
I hope you can work on yourself for the better.
I hope I can too.
I hope we can create something magical.
I know people have been able to emerge
from a harsh past to a beautiful future.
I want that to be with you.
But, I also need to accept that it might not.
Because, if we love each other enough to try again,
we should love ourselves enough to know
when to let go.

## I don't know what you want me to say.

Should I say I'm not scarred?

That I can't even look at photos
of the clean apartment
because I get flash images of the bloody kitchen
or bathroom.

That for days after,
all I could picture was you
hobbling over to show me what you'd done.

That I can't even say what you did
or what happened without crying?

I don't know what you want from me.

The only thing that I feel will come
from communication is more pain.

Every time I think of that night,
I think about how I shouldn't have been
collapsed on the ground on the phone
with the 911 operator
telling me help was on the way.

I was supposed to be at a Christmas party.
I was supposed to be bowling with coworkers.

Not staying at a friend's because I couldn't
be around the blood without hyperventilating.

Not trying to figure out how to clean the apartment
because the entire place was stained crimson.

What good would talking be?
I don't hate you.

I just know for both of our sanity and health,
we need to just stop communicating.

## I don't know why I'm writing to you.

I don't really think I want to.
But I thought it might help me breathe for once.
Part of me wants to know how you're doing.

Like,
How's work?
Did you find a place to live?
Are your friends back home excited
you're coming back?
Are you thinking about going back to school?
Did you actually find a therapist?

Do you,
Do you think about me?
Do you think about how I'm just trying
to protect myself?

Part of me wants to just forget about you.
I want to forget everything that we had.
I want to forget the feeling I had
when I would see you at the café.

The sheer joy and happiness I felt
when I would see you working,
making drinks, talking to the regulars.

How you would simply take my breath away.
How your radiance brought me happiness.

I want to forget it.
I want to forget the happy memories we did share.
Because then that way, this would be much easier.

And no matter,
no matter how much I feel I should hate you.
That I should regret you.
That I should pretend you never existed.
That you never happened.

I can't.

But, it's kind of impossible to forget you now isn't it?
Did you plan that?

Did you plan that you will scar the back of my
mind every time something makes me think of you?

I am a little angry at myself for not hating you.
For hoping you're doing okay.
For hoping you don't try and hurt yourself again.
That you actually get the help you need.
I'm not just protecting myself.
I'm protecting you too.
You need to understand that you need
to find your own inner peace.
I really hope you find that.
I still want you to succeed and follow the dreams
you told me.

There's a frightened child
in that catastrophic mind of yours.
I want to believe that I saw him in there.
He showed me what an amazing man he could be.

Lean on your family and friends.
Love yourself.
And the rest will follow.

But, I will be gone.
I won't be there when you find him.
And don't go looking for me.

No matter how much I want to.
I won't be able to hate you.
But I know you're not healthy for me.
I'm not healthy for you.

# I don't know how I'm the bad guy.

I tried.
I really tried to make this work.
I wanted us to stay friends.
I wanted you to be a part of my life.
But when that put me in danger...
When that harmed my mental health...
When it put you in danger...
I wasn't going to sit there,
pretend nothing happened
and go on with life, letting you dictate it.
I'm suddenly the bad guy.
I'm suddenly the ex-girlfriend who went too far.
When in reality,
I'm the first one to fight back.
I don't know how filing a protection order
was so wrong?
You're still not a criminal.
You can live your life and no one,
I mean no one will need to know.
Yet, I am the bad guy.
But, I can understand.
I understand why your family is blocking me,
unfriending me.

Because they don't want to hurt you.
And believe me.
I don't want that either.
Does it hurt that I will live on by the story you tell?
Yes.
Do I wish I could have shared my side?
Yes.
But they will choose you.
Which I want them too.
There are times I want to scream and shout.
Get my story out.
Have the whole world know what I have
and have been going through.
I am keeping it in so that you don't lose
those close to you.
And because I am not perfect too.
I did some pretty horrible things to you.
I wish I never did.
I wish I never let my emotions get the best of me.
But, I was scared.
I was only trying to protect myself.
Toward the end,
I kept my composure.

Even when you began to crumble.
Even that night.
I still didn't fight with you,
didn't argue with you,
tried to get you to stop,
watched as you reached for the knife,
screamed when I saw your blood,
called 911,
let the police in,
asked if you were still there,
asked if you were still breathing,
asked if you would be okay.
Even as I crumbled to the floor in a heap of tears.
I still hoped and wished you were okay.
I couldn't even breathe that night.
Every breath was torture.
Every moment of silence was a nightmare.
Every touch was terrifying.
And yet all I could do was sit blankly and process
what just happened.
So, how?
How am I the bad guy?

**I really hate how you
still can consume my mind.**

I really want to keep you away
from everyone and everything I love.
It's not fair.
It's not fair that I get banished from your family
and friends, yet you hold on to mine?
How is that fair?
But, I guess what a wise friend told me is true.
That you need all the help you can get.
And my friends are great people
who are willing to help those in need.
Maybe you're doing it out of desperation.
Maybe out of jealousy.
I hate how all I can think about,
all I feel will all be too real,
is what you'll do the first thing you get back home.
You'll hit up all the people who made me so insecure.
Maybe love them up a bit.
Make them feel sorry for you.
Have them make you feel better by fucking you.
And I hate that that's something I still fear.
That's what I fear and worry you'll do
to those close to me.

Just to get back at me.
You already tried.
Hiding away photos of my best friend
for your own enjoyment.
I want to hate you.
But I know I never will be able to.
It hurts to say you meant so much to me before.
Now you're just a ghost that haunts me in my sleep,
the monster in my nightmare.
Now you're the panic behind my panic attacks.
Part of me still hopes we can be friends in the end.
Part of me hopes that once this year is over,
you'll try and reach out.
Only part of me.
The other part of me knows how poisonous
we are for each other.
The other part of me hopes that you'll find help
and move onto someone new.
Part of me hopes that you'll change for the better.
I just hope that new person isn't any of my friends.
But I can't predict the future.
I can't change someone's feelings for another.

I can't keep two people apart from each other
if they are happy together.
As much as it will kill me,
at first.
I know that all I want for you is to be happy.
From the very start,
it's all I've wanted.
So as much as I don't want it to happen,
I can't keep it from happening.
Just stay away from me if you do.

# I think it's odd

how I went from caring too much,
to now not really caring at all.
Is that bad?
Maybe it's good.
I need to move on.
I can't have what you do
or don't do affect me anymore.
And I won't.
I can't have your voice in the back of my head
telling me what I should or shouldn't do.
I'm actually kind of mad, annoyed.
At you,
your family.
Which I think is what I feel is the bad part because,
I shouldn't feel that way.
They didn't do me wrong.
But they think I did, don't they?
It's whatever I guess.
I just hope it makes you change but now....
I feel like now this is just going to make it worse.
I'm sorry.
I tried to help you.
But,
you can only help yourself.

**Can you stop?**

Can you please just leave me alone?
Can you stop keeping me from ever wanting
to date again?
I can't even trust myself.
I can't even trust those around me.
Every time I think that I know what I'm doing.
Doubt starts to creep in and tell me that it's
happening again.
They're going to do exactly what happened before.
Like, why?
Why did you do this to me?
Was this intentional?
Did you mean to burn yourself in the back
of my mind so that I can never trust myself again?
I still get panic attacks.
Did you know that?
I had one today because my friend spilt
red hand sanitizer on her leg.
Red hand sanitizer.
And I couldn't fucking breathe.
When will it stop?
The fear,
the flash backs,
the anxiety?

Maybe I'm just not ready.
But, I also am so sick of you dictating my life.
I am sick of worrying about what you
or your family will think of me for trying to move on.
What I will think about me for trying to move on.
I already think it's going too fast.
I already know that I shouldn't go
too quickly into this.
I know I need to take steps back.
I want to see where this takes me.
And you're not going to be there to fuck it up.

## You were there,

you were there.
I thought you wouldn't be there, but you were.
I felt like I cheated on you.
And all I wanted was you.
As I cried, I wanted you to comfort me.
But that's so fucked up.
I wanted you to tell me everything was okay
and that you loved me.
What a horrible fantasy to have.
I moved too fast.
But part of me feels like I'm the only one
suffering through this.
Did you already sleep with someone?
Was it super easy and simple for you?
Did you shut down and cry afterwards?
Part of me wants to know.
I hate that I still have a love for you.
I want it to disappear.
Someday it will.
But right now, you're consuming me.

## Why can't you just leave me alone?

Even when you're not here, your still everywhere.
Everywhere I go.
Every turn I take.
Every thought.

You're there.

I don't even know what it is.
It's not that you're everywhere
but everything reminds me of you.

I know your birthday is coming up soon.
All I can think about is last year,
how I bought you a cake.
How I got you your favorite sneakers.
How you cried when you saw who was on the cake.
I wouldn't be surprised if those sneakers I bought
you are in a trash somewhere.
Or at a Goodwill.

Sometimes, I wonder if you've already moved on.
I wonder if it was easy.

If she gave you the chances and patience you needed.
If she gave you the motivation to change.
And oddly, I kind of want that for you.
I hope you find someone who is your everything.
I hope you find happiness once you heal yourself.
I hope you can share that happiness with someone new.
That was all I ever wanted for you.
From the very beginning.
I wanted you to be happy.
Even if it wasn't with me.
With that now becoming a reality.
I wonder if it was just that simple to leave me behind.
Recently, I was wondering if I truly gave you
the chances for you to change.
Wondered if I had giving you an ultimatum,
if you'd be here with me right now.

I do miss you.
I miss the happiness and what I thought
was love with you.
I miss being held in your arms,

feeling safe and secure.
I miss hearing the sound of your breath as you slept
next to me.
I miss you kissing my forehead each night
and each morning before work.

I know in your own twisted mind,
you tried to love me.
You tried to have me,
have us, be happy.
But, I think the thing I miss the most
are finding the notes you left me each morning
when things were falling apart.
I ripped up the last ones I found the other day.
I couldn't keep them if I wanted to move on
and grow.
I wish things didn't end up the way they did.
I wish I could have talked to you,
kept you in my life somehow.

Even now I wonder,
when this year is over,
If you'll reach out to me.
Hear that you're doing well,

that you met someone new,
that they became the rock and support you needed.

I shouldn't want that.
I shouldn't miss you.

I still get attacks of anxiety when I see anyone
who remotely looks like you.
I try to find you in every biker I drive past.
I try to find you in every man standing at a bus stop.
I don't understand why I want to know
what you're up to.
What good would that do?

Sometimes I think if I see that you're happy and well,
the pain of seeing you so much better without me,
will help me move past too.

I need to grieve you.
I need to miss you.
I need to want you.
I need to be angry with you.
I need to feel the hurt of you,
for you.

I need to take you as an experience to grow from.
I need to know that I tried.
I did all I could to help you and help us stay together.
I need to love myself,
honor my values,
rebuild myself,
my understanding of love,
and try again.
Try again with someone new.

I hope you do too.

I hope we find our everything.

I hope we were just a bump in the road to our
futures.

I hope you know that I love you.

I loved you.

I need you to know,
no matter who comes in my life next,
you will be a scar I'll need to wear with pride.

You will be at the back of my mind, until I find a new
poison to drink.
A new poison that will blossom into a stronger me.

Good bye,

I will love the small and happy times,
I will grow from the pain,
And I wish you all the best.

Good bye,
You were my first love and hardest heartbreak.

Please promise me to grow,
to change for the next person.
You deserve happiness too.

Everyone does.

Don't let this keep you from achieving that goal.
Even with our broken paths,
I want everything for you.
Good bye, I love you.

## I thought I was done writing to you.

I wrote a freaking goodbye letter to you.

But here I am again.

Why?
I don't know.
I think I just have too much time on my hands now
to think of you.
I don't want you to have this effect on me.
I don't want you to have this hold on me.

You don't deserve it.
You never deserved it.
You don't deserve my tears,
my hurt,
my pain,
after everything you put me through.

You don't deserve my happiness,
my joy,
my excitement,
my love.

You don't deserve any of it.

You hurt me.
You scared me.
You traumatized me that I still get panicky
about that night.

And you can go off and act like it never happened?
Act like I am the one who needs to be blocked
from your life?
I am so tired of you having this hold on me.

Why do I still care about how you are.
Why do I still care about who you fuck.
Why,
why,
why?

I want you out of my fucking head.

If you can do one thing,
one fucking thing for me,
please leave my mind.
Pack your bags and leave.

Leave me be.

I don't want you anymore.

I loved you.
I hurt for you.
And I need to move on from you.

I need to keep growing and exploring and loving me.

Leave me alone.

Please.

If you could ever do one thing for me again.

Leave me be.

**It used to be a longing for you
when I would see a picture of us together.**

Now it's fear.
I'm not sure if that means I'm completely over you
or if I'm seeing you for who you really are.
You are my biggest fear.
My biggest fear since I was a child.
Of being controlled.
Being abused.
Feeling like I have no way out.
Just like how I felt as a child.
I don't ever want that again.
I see the signs.
I know when to leave now.
I want to continue to grow.
I want to continue to set boundaries
that I will not let be crossed again.
Because my definition of love is not what we had.
It unfortunately is all you ever known.
But I know now that's not what I want.
I've known since then it wasn't what I wanted.
I just need to continue to grow
and let those boundaries be my priority.

**I think I get so upset
that there's a piece of you with me.**

probably the only good piece,

the piece of pure life,

pure happiness,

pure genuine love for the music.

Thank you for that,

thank you for showing me a new world of music.

A new world where I feel alive.

I feel the life flowing within,

I feel free.

Should I feel conflicted for that piece of happiness

you brought to me?

Sometimes, I don't want it.

I don't want anything

that can bring me closer to you.

Sometimes, I love it.

I am so glad that through all that pain,

I got some tiny amount of pure joy.

I think my hurt will lessen.

I know it's gotten better.

Recently, it has been harder.

I have so much happening.

So much stressing me to the point

where I fall back to old patterns.

And that, that scares me.
But I need to be soft on myself.
There will be these moments.
Where I will regress instead of progress.
If I am not soft with myself.
I will become stuck.
This is probably the only thing
that I will have stick with me,
the one thing that will remind me
of you for longer than I want.
It will remind me of the love that we had,
that I had for you.
At one point you were my everything.
It's shitty to think that that will never make sense
in your mind.
You have such a twisted view of the world
that anything I do or say will always be against you.
That I never had those feelings for you.
That my dear, will never be true.
I did.
I did love every fucking thing about you.
To the point I lost myself.
I lost my sense of what love truly is.
I recognized that we, what that was, was not love.

I recognized for my own happiness, my own growth.
We needed to let each other go.
We needed nothing to do with one another.
We were poison.
Even through that poison.
There were some moments of happiness.
This music will be that for me.
The times I think that I saw you the most alive.
It's hard for me to piece that you have changed.
That you are better, better to try with someone else.
I hope you did.
I hope this distance between us
put things in perspective.
I will hold this piece of music with me.
No matter how hard I try to push it away.
It's now a piece of me.
It always has.
But now, it has a bit of a hard past.
I'm going to use it for the good.
I'm going to use it for its intended purpose.
I'm going to use it to feel the universe.
To feel the life that's all around us.
To feel free and unbreakable.
To be life itself.

## To the Girl Who Dates You Next...

I hope you're safe.

I hope you see through the deception,
the manipulation
the sweet, sweet lies with smirking kisses.

I hope you respect yourself enough
to know your name doesn't end with
"bitch" or "cunt".

I hope you leave when he throws
something in the apartment the first time.

I hope you know he's trying to control you
when he threatens to hurt you or himself
the first time.

I hope you try hard not to fall into
his poison and start displaying
the same behaviors.

I hope you don't convince yourself
out of calling the police,
when you're afraid,
and crying on the floor.

Most of all,
I hope you know your worth,

you know when to walk away,
you know that you don't deserve this.

You know that this,
this is not love.

That you are not the problem.

I hope that if you are afraid,
scared,
that you talk to someone.

I hope you talk to a friend,
a coworker,
someone passing by,
what's really happening behind closed doors.

Because that's how you'll be able to get out.

How you will be able to escape.

But for now,

I hope you are safe.

## I dated a "healthier" you...

But why?
How did I miss this?
Why did I get so swooped in?

I thought I had broken the cycle.

What happened?

I know I was avoiding.
I was avoiding thinking about the court date.
Thinking about that it was coming up.
Thinking about his new girlfriend.

Is that what brought me there?

It was subtle this time.
Or was I just not looking for the signs?

I think I felt it.
I felt the anxiety and the uneasiness.

But why did I continue?
Why did I think that this time it would be different?

Part of me feels like I failed.
I thought I had done so well.
I thought I did all the right things,
yet I still attracted someone like you.

I think the difference might have been that,
maybe I felt that lover was trying to change.

Maybe that's why it was easier to miss?
Why can't I just let go of you?

I don't even know who I'm talking to anymore.

Am I talking to you?
Am I talking to my mother?
Am I talking to him?

Or am I talking to myself?

I am telling this person,
this thing,
to leave me alone.

I don't want to keep attracting you.

Arlyne, you know the signs.
Don't get hard on yourself for slipping this time.

You were weak,
you were vulnerable,
you were avoiding.

Don't avoid anymore.

Keep working on you and be the lovely
person you are.

You will not keep attracting a "healthier" abuser.
Or persona.

Right now,
even though I had seen you a few months ago,
you feel like a haunting image.

Still chasing me.
Still have a grasp on me.

I'm frustrated I slipped up.

But I can understand why.

I knew before I could sense it.
I could feel it.
I was overwhelmed and drained.
I needed something familiar.

But this time,
this time I wasn't afraid of my safety.
I will always be grateful to lover
for showing me that.

I need to keep working on saying no to the other
unhealthy patterns.

But right now,
be fucking frustrated.
Be hurt,
be angry.
Why can't you just leave me be?

You're a monster,
a haunting image of my childhood torment.

Go away.

Please.

Just go away.

## This doesn't seem right.

This doesn't seem real.
The feelings I feel.
The fear I feel.

I thought I had locked you away for good.
And yet you're here.

You followed me across the country to land
untouched by you.
Land that never experienced your pain,
your trauma.
Land that didn't experience mine...

Yet, it feels like I never left.

It feels like I'm being
chased,
followed,
by your toxicity.

I know I am safe,
but my body doesn't.

My body is warning me
screaming, "this isn't safe."
Telling me I should run.
Pleading that I don't stay.

Yet everywhere around me is safe.

You are not here.
You never were here.
You will never come here.
You will never be able to touch me again.

Yet,
you do.

In the panic attacks,
the flashbacks,
the shallow breathing,
the shaking hands,
the trembling lips,
the shuttering sobs,
my aching being.

You still have a grasp on me.
Like a suffocating shadow.
Slowly taking control of my actions.
Wrapping your dark twisted
hands around my throat,
stealing any air that escapes,
keeping the screams silenced.

All consuming.

I want to spit you out.
Dig into my chest and rip you out.
Reclaim what is mine.

This body deserves healing.

The more I connect,
the more I touch,
appreciate,
honor this body,
this being,
me.

The shadowy hands loosen their grip,
and I'm able to breathe.

I can share my story.
I can calm my wounded,
frightened body.
I can start to release.
Release all this grief,
pain,
hurt.

All that is no longer mine to hold.
All that was never mine to hold.

And,
hopefully soon,
I can completely and fully
release you.

## What are these feelings?

This shame?

That I shared too much
and I need to escape.

It happened when I
talked about you.

The poison in the family.

I had this shame
because maybe I said
too much,
this was all too real
the pain I've been
trying to cover up.

Behind the smiles,
the confidence,
the laughs,
that shame of
my roots and
of you.

You are the poison.

The poison I've
been working hard
to detox from my
system.

And you're still there.

You have my brother
and my sister
and I want them
back.

Give them back,
give them back to me.

Give them back to our
healing family.

They deserve to be happy too.
They deserve the freedom
from your grasp,

they deserve to heal
and grow,
to break the cycle,
to stop the pain,
to heal from the pain,
to ground new healthy roots
and bloom with fiery grace.

They deserve it.
They don't deserve you.
They never deserved you.
And you need to leave.
You need to leave this
family.

Haven't you done enough?

You damaged our relationship
and raised us in trauma.

I lost my sister,
I lost my brother
To the toxicity of your greed.

Your need to continue the cycle,
destroy the love,
damage the nurtured.

Leave my family alone.
Leave me alone.

Please,
Just go.

Find somewhere else to feed.
And let them go.
Let them go.

## There's a song

that brings me
back to you...

to all the pain
the worry
and the fear
you left me in
that you forced
upon me

how you gripped
my chin
as you poured
your toxins
into my body
and I pushed
and clawed
screaming
to let me go
as the water
spilt from my lips
and your hand
just got tighter
and I couldn't move

I couldn't
remove you,
keep you
from filling my lungs
with water
and telling me
that I made it up
that I created this
monster before me

clutching onto me
with bloody claws
and a sneering grin
your eyes burning red
from the demons
within

the one you allowed
to nestle inside me
where he pokes
and prods
telling me what to do

what to say
to keep me his prisoner

you were that poison
you were the creator
and you both watch
me ignite into flame
and place the blame
on the girl who adored
you

and was foolish enough
to think
that if you say
a little prayer
the darkness
inside you
would settle
and the demons
would be free
of you...

Because you are
the poison

you are the reason
I'm still
relearning how to breathe.

I'm still learning
to love the parts of me
you shamed

because you
were afraid of
intimacy
and so was I.

**Even when I**

thought I had
healed from
you

the imprints
your hands
left me
burn
underneath
my skin
before I
even realize
it was you
who came
to visit.

*(when I try to date someone new)*

**My poor body**
can sense
your heart
beating...
and it's
terrifying.

*(go away)*

## I don't know what

to write about
anymore,
to you
or to him.

I see now
that he
was just
an
illusion,
a form
of protection
to keep my
mind at
bay
knowing
you
were
here
to
stay.

**Dear you,**

Just writing your name
makes my soul
shake.

Why am I writing
to you?

Did you know
in the past
month
I've had
two panic
attacks?

I honestly don't
know why
but I
think
you
were
part of it

part of why
I was gasping,

needing to
breathe

uncertain
of my
reality

if I was
here

or back
home

where you
kept me

safe and
sound

keeping my voice
shut and my
face to the
ground

covering my
head

with
my arms
as you
threw
whatever
got in
your
way

how you seemed
to always
make yourself
the victim.

Poor you,
how dare I
not be
satisfied
with a
bed
after
your phone
was thrown
at my head?

How dare I
refuse to
talk to
you
after you
stabbed
yourself
in my
living room?

How dare I
place a
protection
order
after
countless
nights of
screams
telling me
how
I
just
need
to

give
you
more
chances

and that
if I
just
let you
fuck me
we'd be
happily
ever
after

that if
I
just
didn't
have a voice,
didn't have
boundaries
that
this

would
work
out
and
we'd
be
in
love

and
you...
you'd be
my
everything

but
you
know
what
I
say
to
that
dream?

It can
go to
hell

like you
and the
rest of
your
family.

## I feel like I'm holding

a lot of anger

a lot of anger and
hurt from the past
that's affecting my
future

I start to turn inwards
and attack myself
based on the messages
that I was told,

over and over again,
that I need to
make time and
space for you.

For you and
only you

and when I begin
to falter, oh no
all hell breaks
loose because I
need to support
you because I'm the
problem, I always
have been and I
always will be
but the difference
here is, you think
that

I don't.

I don't want to be
defined by the stories
you told because
most of them are
lies and reflections
of the fear inside
of you.

That you cannot
look in the mirror
and accept that
you are flawed
too

that you are your
own worst enemy
and that I
will never be
your punching
bag again.

*(you)*

## Broken hearts

and broken dreams

tears streaming
down your cheeks

you hear the screams
but you are
numb

telling yourself
that you
are not
the one

the one
who is receiving
this pain

the one who is
being thrust open

their sperm leaving
traces on your
skin

it's not you,
it's them

it's someone
else's body
who's
being used
abused
and oh
so torn
inside

that you're
not
sick to your
stomach
and you
can't breathe

so you
close
your
eyes
and pretend

you're
asleep

because
then,
maybe

maybe
this
was always
just
    a
        dream.

*(rape)*

## You stained

my world
with crimson
red roses

so that anyone
who speaks
of love
turned
into
thorns.

**I met you at the**

rose garden today
for the last
time

except it wasn't
you,
it was him

an encapsulation
a representation
of the love
I lost,
the heartbreak
left open
and words
left unspoken

as we talked
I realized that
all this time
it was you

you
lingering through

the shadows
of my heart

twisting the
love I
sought
in others,
in myself.

You
were
there,
the whispers
of grief
through the
air

and I
understood
that even if
this man
before me
was my
soul mate

the smell
of your
fear
will continue
to linger
until
I allow
myself
to
accept,

I truly
loved
you.

I saw
you.

I understood
your pain.

And
watching
you

be
consumed
by your
demons
while hoping
things
will change
is the
pain I
carry

the heartbreak
of my
failure
to not have
pulled
you
with me
to
the light.

*(the rose garden)*

# author's note

Wow, here she be. This work of poetry has taken three years to finally publish and share to you. I was nervous to share these poems due to their rawness, anger, rage, fear, and vulnerability. These poems were my way of processing the traumatic end to an abusive relationship I was in about five years ago. They were all letters to that person, and it had soothed me so much to write down all that I was thinking and feeling in a sporadic and poetic way. I chose not to edit any of the poetry because I wanted the rawness to be felt by you readers. I wanted to share my story and process of working through this trauma in hopes to remind anyone who is processing trauma that they are not alone. Many of us are processing intense and scary memories. Feeling and shaking out the trauma even years after the experience. And, as we move through the pain. Slowly, over time, the triggers will lessen. Your body will relax. People will hold you and love you. And you will come back home to yourself.

This is the first poetry collection of my journey. I will be sharing with you two other books that relate to this process and hope that you enjoy and read them too.

Thank you so much for reading and I hope you enjoyed my little words.

# acknowledgements

Thank you to everyone who has been a part of making this book possible. To my editors, therapists, friends, family, and completely kind and loving strangers. Thank you. This book would not have been possible without you. Thank you for holding me through those challenging first few years and for believing in my little light. I appreciate you all.

## about the author

Arlyne is a menstruating being who writes about this life through art. Arlyne has always found writing poetry as a beautiful, releasing, and creative outlet for her own healing journey. She is a proud Chicana and lives in her now home city of Denver, Colorado with her dear friend Vanessa, Vanessa's son Oliver, and their pets, Koko, Ruby, Jude, and some fish. This is Arlyne's first book.

@tecuani_cihuatl